The American Journalists

ANDREW BRADFORD

Horatio Gates Jones

ARNO
&
The New York Times

Collection Created and Selected
by Charles Gregg of Gregg Press

Reprint edition 1970 by Arno Press Inc.

LC# 79-125699
ISBN 0-405-01678-6

The American Journalists
ISBN for complete set: 0-405-01650-6

Reprinted from a copy in
The New York Historical Society Library

Manufactured in the United States of America

Andrew Bradford,

Founder of the Newspaper Press in the Middle States of America.

AN ADDRESS

DELIVERED AT THE

ANNUAL MEETING

OF THE

Historical Society of Pennsylvania,

FEBRUARY 9TH, 1869.

BY

HORATIO GATES JONES.

Published, with an Introductory Note, in pursuance of a Resolution of the Society.

PHILADELPHIA:

KING & BAIRD, PRINTERS, No. 607 SANSOM STREET.

1869.

INTRODUCTORY NOTE.

OR the last few years the Historical Society of Pennsylvania, it has been noted, has been growing largely in public favor and importance. The munificent bequest of its former Vice President, the Hon. Henry D. Gilpin, and quite recently the testamentary benefaction of Mr. George W. Fahnestock, whose untimely loss the Society yet freshly deplores,—the former an endowment in money and books, the latter in a collection of pamphlets of almost unexampled extent and richness in sources of American History—were among the manifestations to the public generally, more evident than others, less material, of the consideration which the body had attracted of late from scholars and from the lovers of American History. Its meetings are now beginning to be numerously attended; and its proceedings to have interest with the public throughout the State. It is, in fact, at this day an Institution of the Commonwealth of Pennsylvania. It would not therefore have been entirely surprising if the Annual Meeting of February, 1869, had brought together, under any circumstances, a large number both of citizens and strangers. The expectation of a discourse from one of the most valued members of the Society, on a historic character of the Province long connected with its earliest press, was, however, doubtless the specific motive which animated to their attendance, the numerous visitors, both ladies and gentle-men, who filled the Society's halls at the late Annual Meeting. The evening was one, every way, of unusual interest. A fine work of art—a historic picture from the pencil of Mr. Heaton—was presented by Col. JAMES ROSS SNOWDEN, with some eloquent remarks. Many of the curious objects of the museum—including relics of Penn and Washington, rarely brought from the fire-proof repository of the Society—had been produced on this occasion for the view and inspection of strangers. The princi-pal event of the evening was, however, the Annual Discourse. It is now presented with the remarks of the President of the Society, Mr. WALLACE, introducing the speaker.

Having taken the chair at 8 o'clock and called the body to order, Mr. Wallace remarked, that the earliest sketch which had come down to us of the organic plan of the Historical Society of Pennsylvania, made: "a discourse by one of the members," to which "strangers should be admitted," a princi-pal feature of the Annual Meeting. And the earlier printed records of the body contained several papers of this sort which were valuable contributions to the history of the City and Province. The practice had fallen of later years, he believed, into some desuetude, owing, he presumed, to the labor and research required from any one who would present, with ful-ness and accuracy, early historical matters in Pennsylvania, or, indeed, as he supposed, in any of the States of the Union which made the "Old Thirteen."

He was happy to say that on this, the evening of the Annual Meeting for 1869, the Society had the promise of a renewal of the excellent custom which had been contemplated as a perma-nent one by the wise founders of the body. Mr. HORATIO GATES JONES had promised to read to it an essay on an useful and respected citizen of the Province. The Society had been already greatly indebted to Mr. Jones. Some years ago he gave to it a valuable historic sketch of the First Paper Mill built in British America; an essay in which he proved conclusively that the manufacture of paper in America, so important, was first established, not near New York, as the people of that splendid city had been led to suppose, nor yet in New England, as the laudable ambition of our eastern cousins willingly believed, but on the contrary, was established here, in this unpretending region, and in what was now our own incorporated city; its location having been on the banks of the Wissahickon; where, the speaker observed, its foundations yet remained to show its early existence.

On another occasion the Society was indebted to Mr. Jones for an essay upon the services rendered to physical science, and particularly to the science of Electricity by the Rev. Ebenezer Kinnersley, Professor of Oratory and English Literature from 1753 to 1773 in the College of Philadelphia; an interesting and valuable essay, as all who heard it would remember.

The Society was, this evening, to be favored, he understood, with a paper connected with the history of our early printing; a subject of as great intrinsic interest as either of the others referred to, and perhaps more popularly engaging. Without further proem he begged therefore, to introduce to the audience the orator of the evening—well known to them all by good report, though not perhaps to all personally—Mr. Horatio Gates Jones, for many years the Corresponding Secretary of this Society, now one of its Vice-Presidents, and a member of numerous Historical Associations in the United States.

Mr. Jones, being thus introduced by the President, delivered his discourse, the subject of it being Andrew Bradford, who first established the newspaper press in the Middle Colonies. The discourse was listened to with close attention, and the interest of its valuable matter even heightened by the animation with which the speaker delivered it, and by numerous manuscripts, pamphlets and larger books, with which he illustrated the discourse as he went along. At the conclusion of it, Mr. JOHN A. McALLISTER, of the Executive Council, having made some appropriate remarks expressive of the great and renewed obligation under which the Society was to Mr. Jones, offered the following resolutions, which, on motion, were unanimously adopted.

*R*ESOLVED, That the thanks of the Historical Society of Pennsylvania are hereby tendered to HORATIO GATES JONES, Esquire, for his valuable, accurate, and instructive address commemorative of ANDREW BRADFORD, one of the early and useful citizens of our Province, and the founder of the Newspaper Press of Pennsylvania.

*R*ESOLVED, That Mr. JONES be requested to furnish to the Society a copy of his Address, for preservation among the Archives of the Society and for publication.

*R*ESOLVED, That while the newspaper press of Philadelphia, independent, decorous and pure, is a monument worthy of its founder, ANDREW BRADFORD, there is yet due to his services from the men of this generation, some tablet or cenotaph more specially dedicated to his memory; and that the subject of such a memorial is hereby referred to the Executive Council for consideration and future action.

After a report by the Librarian, the Rev. Dr. Shrigley, on the state of the Library, by which it appeared that nearly 50,000 pamphlets had been added to it by the will of the late lamented Mr. Fahnestock, the Society proceeded to the annual election of officers, when the tellers, Mr. Penington and Mr. Stone, reported the gentlemen whose names appear on the third page of the present tract as unanimously elected. After some other business of form the Society adjourned.

ANNUAL DISCOURSE,

1869.

MR. PRESIDENT,

LADIES AND GENTLEMEN:

THE READING of historical essays and papers is prescribed as part of the regular proceedings of the Historical Society of Pennsylvania; but it is a subject in the order of our business which we attempt more rarely than could be desired. The matter has some intrinsic difficulty. In regard to topics which have had much public importance, or in respect to persons who have filled a large space in the eye of their country, everything is already known perhaps to the world, as well as it could be set forth by any speaker who would be willing to address you.

An opportunity for presenting this class of papers, occurs only when some character can be found who,

without having filled any very conspicuous post in
his day, yet occupied, in fact, a respectable place
with credit and usefulness, and who, at the same
time, stood at the humble origin of arts or insti-
tutions which in later years have risen to so great
magnitude as to give interest and dignity to everything connected with their early history—persons,
nevertheless, who, sometimes from one cause and
sometimes from another, and often from the acci-
dental combination of several, may have left for the
general knowledge, little besides their name.

I have selected for the purpose of a plain, but
I trust truthful, historic narrative this evening, the
services of ANDREW BRADFORD, an early citizen of
Philadelphia, whose name was long and largely connected with the now much forgotten history of the
early press of Pennsylvania.

The interest which was exhibited in May, 1863, in
the city of New York, when the great religious cor-
poration of Trinity Church, the Historical Society
of New York, and the municipal authorities of our
sister metropolis, united on the two hundredth anni-
versary of his birth, to do honor to the name of
that eminent printer, William Bradford, and when
the commemorative address was delivered at the hall
of the Union, under the most auspicious circumstances, by the Hon. John William Wallace, now
the respected President of our Society, leads me to

hope that a few words about the less gifted, less enterprising, but not less respectable or less successful son, will not be amiss before this audience.

Andrew Bradford, the son of that William Bradford who first printed in Pennsylvania and New York, was born in Philadelphia in the year 1686. It is probable that he derived his Christian name from his maternal grandfather, Andrew Sowle, of London, an extensive publisher during the Commonwealth and Restoration. In 1693, when seven years old, he went, on the removal of his parents, with them to New York, and in that city, in his father's office, he was taught the art with which his name is connected in Pennsylvania. In those early days of our Province, a classical education was probably not to be obtained in the colonies which now form the Middle States. But, in common with those valuable men who were first born on our soil, and record the transition of its people's birthright from England to America, Bradford received such education as was taught, and it is likely, from parental counsel, those yet better principles of right conduct which lie at the foundation of character, and to which he owed, in earlier life than is common, such offices of trust and profit as were known in the primitive society of Philadelphia. His handwriting, specimens of which are preserved, indicate nothing like illiteracy.

A pamphlet published in New York, with the

imprint of William and Andrew Bradford, shows
that in 1711 he was probably in partnership with
his father; and the publication of the colonial laws
of New Jersey, in 1732, with the same imprint, as
" Printers to the King's Most Excellent Majesty for
the Province of New Jersey," would indicate that
the partnership continued for some years.

In the year 1712, the subject of our sketch removed to Philadelphia, in which city his father had
formerly lived, and where, notwithstanding he had
separated from the Society of Friends, it would
seem he maintained such friendly relations with that
religious sect, as enabled him to secure to his son
a press, of which the Friends were the proprietors.[*]

In the same year, the statutes of the Province
having become somewhat numerous, the Assembly
determined to have the laws printed. As there was,
at that early day, no other competent printer nearer
than New York and Boston, it was probable that
Andrew Bradford was induced, by the prospect of
securing to his press in Philadelphia the patronage
of the Province, in addition to that of the Society
of Friends, to leave New York, and fix himself
permanently in the city of his birth. He had pre-
viously declined an offer from the State of Rhode
Island.

---

[*] See "The Friend," Vol. XVII. pp. 28, 44.

The journals of the Pennsylvania Assembly record, that on the 3d of Twelfth month, 1712, a proposal from him, on the subject of printing the laws, was read in the House, and a committee having been chosen on the 10th of that month to contract "with such printer as they shall think fit to print the laws," an arrangement was soon after concluded with him. An estimate furnished to the House for composition and press work of the book, exclusive of paper, &c., was 100*l.*; and 50*l.* of the Province stock was placed in the hands of seven persons, who, with the Speaker, were appointed to superintend the publication and to procure five hundred copies of the works when finished. The order concluded as follows:

"What it amounts to more by a true account of the whole "expense and one credit given for the sales made of the same "books, produced to the Assembly for the time being, the same "shall be a debt chargeable on this Province, to be paid out of "the public stock thereof."

The faith of the Province being thus pledged to sustain his enterprise, Bradford soon afterwards issued the work, well known to the profession in Pennsylvania as "Bradford's Laws of 1714," a folio volume of 184 pp. It bears the following title: "*The Laws of the Province of Pennsylvania, collected into one volume, by order of the Governor and Assem-*

bly of the said Province. Printed and sold by Andrew Bradford, in Philadelphia, 1714." The advertisement to the reader informs him that "all the laws made and in force are printed at large, and the titles only of those that are repealed, expired, or obsolete, with the times when they were enacted, are set down in their proper order, whereby such as would have recourse thereunto may with more certainty apply to the originals or the record where they are entered." In consequence, however, of the action of the Queen and Council, who entertained, it is known, constant jealousy of the colonial legislation, many of the acts thus "printed at large" were repealed in England, and became of no more value than those of which "the titles only were set down" in their proper order. The publication, which was a considerable enterprise, became, of course, unsaleable, and Bradford having represented the case to the Assembly, an honorable recognition of the fact was made by that body, with a compensation of 30*l.* for the loss he had incurred.

Bradford was afterwards appointed "Printer to the Province." Careful research has failed to ascertain the year when this monopoly was granted, but he held the place until 1730. In 1728, the legislation of the colony having become more settled with the accession of the Georges, Bradford again published, by order of the General Assembly, the Laws of the Province. This publication, which contains 352 pages, was, like the last, in folio. Both volumes are books of authority, and both were creditable to the state of the Art at that day. It is known that a careful collation was made for the edition of 1714 with the original rolls; and I am not aware that the edition of 1728 is less correct. Of course, they are now referred to more in the history of our Law than in its practice; although in them are also found many enactments still in force in this State.

From 1712 to 1723, when Keimer came here, Andrew Bradford was the only printer in Pennsylvania. His office at this time was in Second street, at his paternal sign of the Bible. Attached to it he had a large store. His earlier advertisements show that commerce in our city was in a very elementary state for the first third of the eighteenth century. In common with the advertisements of all the "great merchants" of the time, they announce an assortment (mostly imported) of things seemingly quite incongruous. "Jesuit's bark, very good Bohea tea, chocolate, molasses, new rice, pickled sturgeon, Spanish snuff, dressed deer skins, superfine lampblack (made at his own factory) and beaver hats, some with silk linings."* As the wealth of the Province increased and its advancing civilization encouraged the outlay,

---

* See Keimer's Gazette, No. 8. Pennsylvania Journal, No. 1238 and 1297.

they show a better kind of enterprise, and after 1730 announced "choice parcels of stationery lately imported from London, Dutch quills, blank books, royal, medium,· demy and post paper, good slates, choice ink powders and japanned ink, sealing-wax and wafers, including crown and half crown wafers for offices, folio letter cases, *very* good paper, as royal demy, superfine large post, foolscap, *gilt paper* for letters,* *fine* glass ink fonts, *very nice* ink-stands of various sorts, and most kinds of stationery ware."

A considerable book store and book bindery for binding his own publications, and such work as the citizens of that day needed, were connected with his press, and formed part of his large establishment.

But the name of Andrew Bradford deserves a place in the history of the Province, more durable than that which it could derive from any of the incidents already mentioned. His father, William Bradford, established the first printing press known in the Middle States. The subject of this sketch, following in the footsteps of his enterprising father, founded the first newspaper. On Tuesday, December 22, 1719, he issued the first number of the *American Weekly Mercury*, a journal which he conducted with

---

* The importation of *gilt paper* indicates that the Province was growing in wealth and increasing in attention to points of elegance and etiquette. The use of this sort of paper for elegant or special correspondence was formerly considered quite a matter of propriety, as much so as the use of wax or the monogram now is.

profit to the close of his life, a term of twenty-three years. It announces its general object to be "the encouragement of trade." Local news, obituary notices, and personal literature, which now occupy and often abuse so large a space of our public papers, appear to have had but small room given to them in the *Mercury.* Foreign news, commercial statistics, custom-house entries, including those of all considerable ports along the coast, and especially of New York and Boston, took their large and regularly allotted space; and there are occasional literary communications and extracts from English classics. Until May 25, 1721, John Copson, a bookseller, seems to have been connected with Bradford in its sale; but after that date his name disappears from the imprint,* which becomes "*Philadelphia; printed and sold by Andrew Bradford at the Bible, in Second street, and also by William Bradford, in New York, where advertisements are taken in.*" His father's

---

* Mr. Thomas, in his History of Printing, Vol. II., pp. 325–6, gives the following account of this paper: "It was printed on a half sheet of post; but occasionally appeared on a whole sheet from types of various sizes, as small pica, pica and English. It was published weekly, generally on Tuesday, but the day of publication was varied. In January, 174⅞, the day of the week is omitted; and it is dated from January 13 to January 27. After this time it was conducted with more stability

"In No. 22, two cuts, coarsely engraven, were introduced, one on the right, the other on the left of the title; the one on the left, was a small figure of Mercury bearing his caduceus; he is represented walking, with extended wings; the other is a postman running at full speed. The cuts were sometimes shifted, and Mercury and the postman exchanged places.

"The Mercury of December 13, 1739, was 'Printed by Andrew and William

name had appeared as early as June 9, 1720, in No. 26.

In April, 1728,[*] Andrew Bradford, succeeding it is probable Mr. Henry Flower, was appointed postmaster to the Province of Pennsylvania, an office which he held until October, 1737. But concerns of a public character did not withdraw his regards from his art, nor deaden his interest in either it or the literature of his country, which, in the humble manner of his literary abilities, he endeavored to spread, improve, and perpetuate. Having removed his establishment and Bible in 1738 to a more commodious place, No. 8 South Front street, (a place owned and occupied as a printing office for nearly a century afterwards by his great nephew and great great nephew, Thomas and William Bradford,) then the business centre of Philadelphia, he issued, in 1741, the first number of "The American Magazine or Monthly Review of the Political State of the British Colonies," a work for which the time was not yet ready, and which, like a rival enterprise

---

Bradford,' and September 11, 1740, it had a new head, with three figures well executed; on the left was Mercury; in the centre a town, intended, I suppose, to represent Philadelphia; and on the right, the postman on horseback.; the whole formed a parallelogram, and extended across the page from margin to margin. This partnership continued only eleven months when the Mercury was again printed by Andrew Bradford alone. The typography of the Mercury was equal to that of Franklin's Gazette."

[*] Mr. Thomas says, 1732 : It is true that his title of Postmaster does not appear

undertaken by Franklin in the same year, was discontinued after a short experience. Andrew Bradford's work, under the same name which he gave it, was revived by his nephew, Colonel William Bradford, in the year 1757. But all the early magazines had, like some of our own day, a short existence. It has been reserved for Peterson, Arthur and Godey, and last for Lippincott to give us a permanent literature through this class of publications. Almanacs seem to have been a sort of literature more congenial to the taste of Philadelphians in that day. Of these Bradford published not less than seven, viz., Taylor's, Jerman's, Burkett's, Leed's, Titan's, Poor Robert's, Poor Will's, (rivals of Poor Richard's) besides, at one time, a large sheet almanac.

Independently of a more direct good influence upon the humble literature of those days, Bradford deserves respectful commemoration for his early lead in the way of importations from England, which were at least diffusing the savor of humanity and taste. While others are announcing* in horrid as in fit conjunction, "Lately imported, very likely *negro men, boys and girls; rum,* sugar and molasses," his advertisements are of "*gilt* paper for letters, *fine* glass ink founts, and *very* nice ink-stands; Lillie's

in his imprint till June 29, 1732, but see the Weekly Mercury of April 4, 1728; where it is said that ' the Post Office will be kept at the house of Andrew Bradford.'
* Weekly Mercury, No. 768.

Grammars; Boyer's French Grammar, and Coles' English Dictionary; VIRGILII MARONI Opera, Specta-
tors, Tatlers and Guardians, of Bibles of several
sizes, and large and small Common Prayers, of the
Whole Duty of Man, Bishop Beveridge's Private
Thoughts, and the Life of God in the Soul of
Man;" and in 1736, before the Province was willing to support the enterprise, he was trying to raise
the religious contemplation of Friends to something
more spiritualized than their mere material subjects,
by publishing, in handsome octavo, Fenelon's Dis-
sertation on Pure Love, with the Letters of Madame
Guion.*

The severe censorship of the press by the provincial
government, of which Mr. Wallace has spoken so
ably and fully in his address at New York, commemorative of the elder Bradford,† and of which Mr.
David Paul Brown, in his *Forum*,‡ has also given
some account, by no means ended with the earliest
times of Pennsylvania. "We find," says Mr. Brown,§
"that in 1721 the finances of Pennsylvania having
fallen into great disorder, some one had published a
pamphlet entitled, 'Some Remedies Proposed for
Restoring the Sunk Credit of the Province.' Andrew

---

* Weekly Mercury, Nos. 882, 893, 1149.
† Bradford Centenary, pp. 49–60.
‡ The Forum, vol. 1, p. 271.
§ Ib., p. 283.

Bradford was now publishing his *American Weekly Mercury*, and one of the persons in his office inserted in the number of January 2, 1721, the following paragraph on the same subject:

"'Our General Assembly are now sitting, and we have great 'expectations from them, at this juncture, that they will find 'some effectual remedy to revive the dying credit of this 'Province, and restore us to our former happy circumstances.'

"On the 21st of February, 1721, Bradford was summoned for this short paragraph before the Provincial Council. Declaring that he knew nothing of the printing or publishing of the pamphlet, and that the paragraph in the *Mercury* was inserted by his journeyman, who composed the said paper, without his knowledge, and that he was sorry for it, &c., he escaped having his press stopped or being himself prosecuted; but he did not escape without a charge from the Governor, for the future ·not to publish anything relative to or concerning the affairs of this government, or any other of his Maiesty's colonies, without the permission of the Governor or Secretary for the time being.

"He was dealt with more severely and made a much more vigorous stand a few years afterward. It being near the time of the annual elections, a communication was inserted in his journal on the tendency of power to perpetuate itself, and on the necessity of what has since come to be a favorite and familiar doctrine, occasional rotation in office. It forms No. 31 of the *Busy Body*, a series of essays begun by Franklin, in Bradford's *Mercury*, and afterwards continued by different hands. It was well written, and though bold in parts, an air of pleasantry took from it much aspect of malignity. Indeed the whole piece is subdued, below the standard even of orthodoxy in modern democratic politics, and contains much which deserves and would receive at all times, the admiration of every party. It was as follows:

"'To be friends of liberty, firmness of mind and public spirit 'are absolutely requisite; and this quality, so essential and 'necessary to a noble mind, proceeds from a just way of think-'ing that we are not born for ourselves alone, nor our own 'private advantages alone, but likewise and principally for the 'good of others and service of civil society. This raised the 'genius of the Romans, improved their virtue, and made them 'protectors of mankind. This principle, according to the 'motto of these papers, animated the Romans—Cato and his 'followers—and it was impossible to be thought great or good 'without being a patriot; and none could pretend to courage, 'gallantry, and greatness of mind, without being first of all 'possessed with a public spirit and love of their country."

"The motto was from Lucan—

"'Hæc duri immota Catonis secta fuit,
Servare modum, finemque tueri;
Nec sibi sed toto genitum se credere mundo.'

"The editor had observed the free language of the communication, and, in presenting it, says that it was too good to be concealed, that he had repeatedly invited the learned and ingenuous to his assistance, and *given proper caution to his correspondents,* but that, not wishing to take credit for any others' labors, he published this piece unaltered.

"'When it appeared, the Governor made a special summons of the Council to lay the matter before them. Bradford was ordered to be immediately taken into custody, examined by the Mayor and Recorder of the City, and that his *dwelling-house* and printing office *be searched* for the written copy of said libel, so that the author be discovered, and that the Attorney-General commence a prosecution against the said Bradford, for printing and publishing the same.'* He was accordingly committed to prison, and bound over to the court. His paper of the following week, referring to the article, says it was supposed that enough had been said to introduce it without blame; that notwithstanding this it had given offence undesigned. It thinks that the matter had been misrepresented to the persons who conceived the rigorous usage necessary and aggravated. However, it gives a second article on the same subject, and, with some independence, declares that it had been written and was ready for press before the other was printed, and that it had not been enlarged,

---

* Minutes of the Provincial Assembly Vol. III. p. 392. Weekly Mercury, No. 506.

lessened, or altered, for what had happened upon publishing the other. What became of the case finally does not appear, but Bradford made no further apology or submission.* No interruption of his press or paper took place, and it had so good an effect on his reputation that he was soon afterwards elected a councilman of the city of Philadelphia. He continued to hold this honorable position for the residue of life, a term of fifteen years. He was also elected a vestryman of Christ Church, an office, at that time especially, of high dignity, and generally conferred on men of the first social standing. To this responsible post he seems also to have been constantly reappointed as long as his health enabled him to attend to its duties.†

"From this date some fixed ideas, originating from the press itself, began to be had about its liberty in Pennsylvania, and we find both newspapers and pamphlets commenting on the concerns of Government with far greater freedom than they had done before."

Mr. Brown, in paying, as he does, the highest compliment to Andrew Hamilton's defence in New York of Zenger at a later date, shows clearly that

---

* Weekly Mercury, No. 507.

† He was elected a vestryman of Christ Church on Easter Monday, April 11, 1726. The records show his re-election for eleven years, but after that term and until his last illness or death, they are wanting. His election to the City Councils of Philadelphia, was on the 3d ⌣. October, 1727.

Hamilton had learned these doctrines concerning the liberty of the press from the printers Bradford, on the soil of Pennsylvania.

Andrew Bradford was twice married; in the latter instance in 1740, and, it is said, not very happily, to a lady of New York, named Cornelia Smith. She was remarkable for beauty and talents, but not so much so for the amenities which give to female charms their crowning grace. By a testamentary disposal of his considerable property he made, however, a liberal provision for her support. He died, after an illness of some time, on the night of the 24th of November, 1742, aged 56 years, and is interred in the burial-ground of Christ Church, in our own city, of which ancient and honored parish he was long a useful and active member. In Dr. Dorr's history of that church Bradford's name appears, in 1729, as one of the largest contributors to the completion of the church edifice.

His death is announced in Franklin's *Pennsylvania Gazette*, and his own paper, which his widow conducted after his death, was suspended a week on the event, and appeared for the six following weeks in emblems of mourning.

Andrew Bradford appears to have been a practical, active, and useful man, of essential probity, well-regulated temper, and steady habits. His attention was given almost entirely to the sober interests of life, and to its important duties, and by industry, prudence, and integrity, says Mr. Thomas, in his History of Printing, "he increased his property, became easy in his circumstances, and preserved, in a considerable degree, the confidence of his fellow-citizens." I believe that he left no male issue, and that the name in his line expired with him.

The name of Andrew Bradford, and the character. of his newspaper also, has descended to the common knowledge of our time, chiefly through the Autobiography of Dr. Benjamin Franklin, between whom and the elder Bradfords, through several generations, there was a hostility well-known to their contemporaries—both in matters of personal interest and on questions of Provincial and Revolutionary politics. [The speaker having given some account of these, not entirely creditable to Franklin, proceeded:]

If any question had ever come from a dispassionate source as to Bradford's having been bred to his profession, or of either his sufficient editorial capacity or his understanding of the mechanical parts of his art, it is answered by the issues which yet remain of his press. His *Weekly Mercury*, running through a long course of twenty-three years, speaks for itself. For the time of day when it was undertaken, this journal was creditable to the man whose enterprise planned and whose skill conducted it. Its foreign intelligence was various, full, and extensive, and

brought before the colonists of America, with surprising regularity, the politics not only of London
and Paris, but those of Rome, Vienna, and St.
Petersburg; illustrating important battles, as that at
Phillipsburg, reported in the *Mercury* of October 17,
1734, with diagrams, not then, as now, made from
wood and easily.

Its domestic items were accurate, its occasional
communications and its few obituaries good. It
gave early, full and accurate reports of such proceedings of the Colonial Assembly as the Government in its control of the press of that day allowed
to be published. After the office of Postmaster to
the Province gave to Bradford the opportunities of
acquiring the most recent intelligence in the neigh-
boring colonies, his paper contained it regularly and
well-presented. In its mechanical department the
Mercury was in advance of the state of the art in
America. The paper on which it was printed was
good.* Its type (which included a font of German)†
was legible, and as the letters and cuts wore out they
were manifestly replaced with new assortments. Indeed it is evident that many of its cuts were made
expressly for it and for single advertisements. These,

---

* It was chiefly of American manufacture, made at the celebrated Rittenhouse
Paper Mill in Roxborough, the first paper mill ever erected in America.

† See Nos. 928, 1014, 1020, 1083.

it is true, were not elegant, but they show how early
Andrew Bradford led the way to this art in America,
and they deserve to be remembered as evidences of
his skill and enterprise.* How far Bradford was in
advance of his time may be seen by a comparison of
his *Mercury* with the thirty-nine numbers which remain of *Keimer's Universal Instructor.* When Franklin
established his paper—the *Pennsylvania Gazette*—the
Bradfords had been for nearly half a century before
him leading the way to literature and art. And it
was only after their well-planned and indefatigable
labors had cleared away the obstructions which
proved impassable to all less generous enterprise,
that the celebrated representative of their common
art appeared in the field, to gather, along with them,
the fruits of their long-continued toil. His enterprise was confessedly rival. His materials of all
kinds were newly imported from England, and he
was supported by the name and capital of the elder
Meredith, whose son was engaged with him in their
common though unsuccessful attempt to break down
the only man who had been able to resist them. It
is after this that Mr. Thomas, a candid and competent judge, by way of describing the external character

---

* See No. 747 for curious cuts of Liberty and Prosperity, and also Negro Boys;
No. 766 for the 'sign of Paracelcus' Head, over against the prison;' No. 768, Three
Negroes; No. 771, one of " News;" Nos. 787 and 789, Runaways; No. 832, Sign of
the Black Boy; and No. 1045, a Hair Dresser's Sign.

of Bradford's enterprise, says: "The typography of
the *Mercury* was equal to that of Franklin's *Gazette*."*
Mr. Thomas is correct. Any person who is accus-
tomed to the details of a printing office, will see that
there is no difference in the character of the composition, the *Mercury* being set up just as well as the
Gazette. At the origin of the rival journal, when its
printers' balls were new, clean, and soft, and its
press supplied with ink freshly brought from London, the *press-work* of the new journal was better.
But even the ownership of Franklin was no proof
against wear and tear and dirt, nor against the usual
results of them. When his rollers became hard
and dirty, they took the ink unequally, like other
rollers long in use, and "friars" and "monks" appear
to have as little dread of the man who "belonged to no
religion," as of the other more reverential, who
worshipped all his days in Trinity or Christ Church.
Independently of their newspapers, many issues of
both presses yet remain, of which a comparison may
be made. The edition of Bradford's Laws of 1714,
not as well printed as that of 1728, is but little
inferior to one of the very best of his rival's books,
the Lower County Laws, printed thirty-eight years
later, when the art itself was greatly more advanced,
and when the wealth of the Province and the increase

---

* History of Printing, Vol. II, p. 326.

of population had brought a certain return for ornamental outlay. The same relative result will appear by comparing any other volumes which have the imprint of their respective offices.

It is, indeed, a striking fact, and one indicative of the excellence, not to say the superiority, of Bradford's press, that, although Bradford was an active and devoted Churchman, and apparently in no respect specially sympathetic with the tastes or habits of the Society of Friends, (from whom, indeed, his father, with a large body of the early colonists of Pennsylvania, had separated with expressions of some asperity,) this Society, which was the most liberal and most enlightened and most constant patron of printing in Philadelphia, should have always supported him against all other rivals, including Franklin, who in so many respects conformed to their discipline and tastes. "Some few works," says that accurate investigator, Mr. Nathan Kite, lately deceased, whose position as the keeper of the records of the ancient Arch street Meeting, gave him special advantages in examining such subjects, "were printed by Franklin and others, but Andrew Bradford did almost all the printing of the Society till his death in 1742."*

In its literary department the *Weekly Mercury* was creditable and not inferior to the *Pennsylvania Gazette.*

---

* The Friend, Vol. XVII., p. 45.

Like all newspapers of that day, neither journal contained much that was either editorial or communicated. Contrary to what might be supposed, Franklin wrote but little for his own journal. The best of his newspaper compositions, the different numbers of "The *Busy Body*," appeared, as is known, in Bradford's *Mercury*, and many articles published in his own paper and reputed to be his, possess so little merit of any sort, that Mr. Sparks and others best acquainted with his writings, have doubted whether they were his.*

In many instances the literary merits of the two papers are brought into immediate comparison by articles from week to week responding to each other. Those in the *Mercury* are generally equal to those in the *Gazette*; sometimes above them in vigor and never inferior to them in propriety. While others, unwilling to be "too nice" in the choice of what they put before their readers, were ready, in order to promote its circulation, to make their paper the medium of a cynic philosophy, Bradford is entitled to our better praise. Not reposing in "the contempt of silence," which, he says, "might be sufficient for such avowals, he declares to the world as the noble object of his aspiration, meditations which have a tendency to

---

* Franklin's Works, Boston, 1840. Vol. II. pp. 278, 285, *n. n.*

raise and refine human kind; to remove it as far
as possible from the unthinking brute; to moder-
ate and subdue men's unruly appetites; to remind
them of the dignity of their nature; to awaken
and improve their superior faculties and direct them
to their noblest objects."*

Andrew Bradford, as we have said, is buried in
the grounds of Christ Church, to which parish he
belonged, but no monument survives to record the
resting-place of this benefactor to our city and State—
the father of its newspaper press. Is this creditable
to our Commonwealth, to our city, to our typo-
graphical societies, or even to our Historical Society?
We owe to his memory some memorial which
should invite the "passing tribute" which is as-
suredly his due. The character of the worthy dead
deserves protection as much as that of the worthy liv-
ing. Their virtues were as sterling as ours. They
lived, and labored, and toiled amid difficulties unknown
by us of the present age, and as they achieved their
victories under circumstances which would cause
many a one to fail, so their examples should never
cease to animate all who come after them. A beau-

---

* See No. 763, (August 15, 1734,) where Bradford censures with dignified moral
sense some irreverent and vulgar communications in the *Pennsylvania Gazette* of the
1st and 8th preceding. The editor of that paper had inserted them, as he tells
his readers, because "by being too nice in the choice of little pieces sent him by
correspondents, he had almost discouraged them from writing to him any more."

tiful cenotaph erected by the piety of our own day, now marks the spot where long laid unhonored all that was mortal of Godfrey, the inventor of the quadrant. The genius of Fulton is soon to receive, in the grounds of Trinity, New York, from a juster posterity, a monument which his own day had not the taste or the gratitude to erect. While in the highly civilized countries of Europe, even centuries are no bar to honors justly due. The Martyrs' Memorial at Oxford, the Monuments to Dante at Florence, no longer now "ungrateful;" the costly erection at Venice, near three centuries after his death, to the great master of the Venetian school, the immortal Titian—whose paintings everywhere around, one would say were monument enough; and the statues of Gutenberg and Faust in the cities which claim their birth, tell us that it is ever time to pay to departed services and worth, the tribute of public acknowledgment and praise.

Why, then, should not some memorial, even at this late day, be raised to the founder, in this city, of that great source of intelligence, the *newspaper press*, which now exercises an influence more extensive than any other efforts of the art?

True it is that neither statue, nor urn, nor cenotaph can add to the real fame or the intrinsic merit of Andrew Bradford, and so long as the press of Philadelphia occupies the high position it does, and

wields its mighty power on society at large—so long
as our newspapers are circulating their copies by
hundreds of thousands every day, penetrating the
mansion of the rich and the cottage of the poor—
giving to all alike, not only the current literature
of the day, and every important event that hap-
pens in the most distant parts of our country, but
in the same issue enabling us also to know what
is actually occurring in London, and Paris, and St.
Petersburg—so long is the press of Philadelphia
his monument. But the other sort of tribute is
due as well, and this day should discharge a duty
of which no earlier one has been able to feel in
the vast powers of that press, so high an obligation.

Philadelphia Anno 1725

Province of Pennsylvania Dr

To 14 Quires Paper from the 18th December
    to the 10th of August at 2/ - - - — 1:8:0

To 1 Blank Book - - - - - - - - 0:3:0

To 1¼ Sheet of the Laws for the year 1724
    at 28/ ℔ Sheet - - - - — 2:2:0

To Quills Ink and an Almanack - - - - 0:2:1

To 1 Quire Demy Paper - - - - - 0:8:6

To 8 Sheets of the Laws for the year
    1725 at 23/ ℔ Sheet - - - — 11:4:0

                          15:2:7

To Printing the Votes and Proceedings of the
House what the Honourable House please

allowed to make Even   17:5
                        16th — " — "

Errors Excepted ℘ me
This 12 Day of August 1725

                     Andrew Bradford